THE LITTLE BOOK OF PERSUASION

UPDATED

Publishing

Published in England
by GWiz Publishing
Oakhurst, Mardens Hill,
Crowborough, E. Sussex.
TN6 1XL

Tel (+44) 1892 309205

First published 2004
Second Edition 2014
Third (Updated) Edition 2017
Fourth (Updated) Edition 2018

Cover illustrations and 'Walter' character by
Rob Banbury
All illustrations © 2017

ISBN: 978-0-9548800-9-5

CONTENTS

ACKNOWLEDGEMENTS

To the thousands of people who have added to this book with their ideas and questions in coaching and training sessions.

And finally, to all those people out there who have tried to persuade us to do things in the past. You have all been great teachers!

HOW TO USE THIS BOOK

All the ideas in this book can be used ethically and some could probably be used unethically.

The point is: ideas and techniques are simply ideas and techniques! In and of themselves they are not inherently good/bad, positive/negative or helpful/unhelpful. However, the application of them can become ethical or indeed manipulative. Be careful of manipulation! Be careful of trying to meet your own needs without attending to the needs of others.

We encourage you to seek true win/win solutions with others, so that you both get what you want... and are both happy with the results you achieve... and for the relationship you build.

PREPARING
YOURSELF

PERSUASION OR MANIPULATION?

Consider the difference between persuasion and manipulation. Are you just trying to get your own way or find a way that has something for everyone?

Manipulation, when found out, breaks trust and makes it harder to persuade next time.

SELL, SELL, SELL!

Persuasion is a form of selling, where
you are selling ideas.
Watch effective sales people and work
out how they do it.

*Effective persuaders learn from sales people
and adapt their approaches.*

YOU <u>ARE</u> WORTH IT

Work on enhancing your self-esteem
and confidence.
Accept that you <u>are</u> worth it.

*People with higher confidence find it easier
to ask for what they want without
embarrassment or self-deprecation.*

YOU DESERVE IT

Convince yourself beforehand that you <u>do</u> deserve to achieve the result you want.

When people do not truly believe in themselves and what they want, they are less likely to get it because the other person may not see its importance.

MAKE NO EXCUSES!

It is most likely that someone who
started with *less than* you has achieved
more than you want now!
So, let go of internal excuses...
and get curious about new plans and
possibilities.

*Effective persuaders don't make excuses
to themselves...
they have a go... and then another...*

WHO ARE THE BEST?

Consider the key people who have
influenced you in your life.
What did they do? How did they
persuade you and others?

*The most successful people learn from the
best that others have to offer them.*

FIND A ROLE MODEL

If you meet or know others who are persuasive, model yourself on them. Do exactly what they do and act exactly as they act.

When you model yourself on someone completely, you'll get the results they get.

WHY DO THEY DO THAT?

We always have a reason for doing the things we do (even when we do unhelpful or unreasonable things like overeating, arguing and breaking speed limits!)
Why might the other person be doing what they do?

An effective persuader understands the reasons and motivations behind the other person's behaviours.

NOW FOR SOMETHING COMPLETELY DIFFERENT

You may have to take a different approach and try something new.

If you always do what you always did, you'll continue to get what you've always got!

STR-R-R-ETCH

Make sure you have a range of
approaches for getting what you want.

*The person that is most flexible will often
be the most successful.*

CHOICE ALWAYS EXISTS

No matter the situation, you will
always have a choice
in how to get what you need...
all you have to do is get creative and
find the options!

*Effective persuaders make sure they have
options and hence... choices.*

VOYAGE INTO THE UNKNOWN

Sometimes, you may need to take a risk or a step into the unknown in order to be persuasive.

The most effective persuaders are prepared to take calculated risks and learn from the results.

DO YOUR HOMEWORK

The more you know and understand about a situation, the more people treat you as an expert.

If faced with a number of options, people will usually be persuaded by whoever seems to have the highest expertise.

WHAT DO YOU WANT?

Be clear about exactly what you want from the situation and where appropriate what your rights are.

Clarity breeds certainty. Certainty increases persuasion.

BUILD IN CONTINGENCIES

Have your facts straight beforehand and plan for the unexpected. Talk your plan through with a friend.
During persuasion, if the other person throws a curveball, you may have to back off, re-plan and return to it later.

A good plan and back-up plan increases confidence.

DO YOU FEEL LUCKY?

Luck is being in the right place at the right time and being ready for it. It is the point where opportunity and preparation meet.
Can you prepare? Yes.
Can you generate opportunities? Yes
So now you can be lucky!

Luck is actually about increasing your opportunities and being ready for them when they happen.

POWER

What power do you have?
Can you make their life easier
(or more difficult)?
Do you know things they don't know?
Do you have access to things
they don't have access to?
Do you have something
they might need?
Do they have a deadline that you are
not affected by?

The effective persuader understands the power on both sides but takes care not to abuse their power.

WHAT ARE THEY SUPPOSED TO DO?

As well as being clear about what you want, consider what you want the other person to do as a result of your persuasion. Can they actually do it in the timeframe you want?
Also, what will they get out of it? What (if anything) are you prepared to offer them?

The effective persuader also plans their approach from the other person's point of view.

WHAT DO THEY KNOW?

Consider what the other person knows
about your idea.
And what resources do they have that
would help them carry out your
idea/suggestion?

*People tend to do the best they can with the
knowledge and resources available to them.
(This doesn't excuse another person's
behaviour, but may help explain it!)*

SAY IT OUT LOUD

Write down what you want to say and
test it by saying it out loud to someone
you trust. How does it sound?
Ask that person to say it to you. Does it
sound reasonable? Does it say what
you actually want to say?

*Words sometimes sound better in your
head than they do when they come out of
your mouth!*

CREATE THE RIGHT SETTING

Make sure there are no distractions or interruptions for you and the other person. E.g. switch off the TV, take them to a quiet place.

Taking action to create the right setting shows the other person the importance of your message.

CLEARING THE HURDLES

THE TIME AND PLACE

Rather than springing an idea on
someone (when they may not be in a
receptive state),
you might say something like:
"There's something important I want to
talk to you about...
when would be a good time?"

*Effective persuaders create the 'space and
time' to present their idea.*

COUNTER OBJECTIONS

Think about what their objections
might be.
Take the objections one by one and find
ways to counter them.

*If you can deal with their objections, they
are more likely to accept your idea.*

ASSESS THE SEESAW

Write down a list of reasons why they might reject your idea. Then write down the reasons they might accept your idea.
If a person's resistance outweighs their desire to accept your idea, you are unlikely to persuade them.

Everyone has an internal seesaw with resistance on one side and desire/motivation on the other.

THERE IS NO RESISTANCE...

What if there was no such thing as
resistance but simply
attraction to an alternative?
If someone appears resistant to your
idea, find out what
they *are* attracted to instead.
What is attractive to them about the
alternative...
and could you give them this as well
with your own proposal?

*Effective persuaders seek to utilise the real
needs of another person in order to unlock a
stalemate.*

I HAVEN'T GOT TIME

If someone tells you that they "don't
have time" to help you,
perhaps they don't see your
request/idea as a priority.
Consider how it *could be* a priority in
their eyes.

*People are motivated by what they see as a
priority.*

WHAT DO THEY HAVE TO LOSE?

Consider what the other person might lose or lose out on if they actually <u>accept</u> your idea.
You will need to replace this loss with something else.

The best persuaders arrange it so that as well as getting what they want for themselves, the other person comes away with more than they started with.

ALTERNATIVE SOLUTIONS?

What if you can't persuade them?
What will you do then?
Is there another way of achieving what
you want?

*Having an alternative plan gives you more
confidence and prevents you from seeming
desperate!*

WHO ELSE COULD HELP?

If the other person won't listen to you, who else might they listen to?

The effective persuader will check to see if they are the best person for the job. If someone else has more credibility, they may persuade that person to help.

TAKE A TIME-OUT

If you start feeling particularly
uncomfortable or sense that they feel
uncomfortable, back off!
Either come back to it later, or change
your approach.

*The successful persuader will trust their
intuition and not just keep on going when
their approach is not working.*

HANDLE THEIR CONCERNS

Explain clearly what you want to achieve and allay any fears the other person may have by listening to and discussing their concerns.

People feel more confidence in an idea when they can see their concerns are being treated sensitively, especially if they are then resolved.

STEP INTO THEIR SHOES

If the other person has doubts and isn't
"buying" your idea, ask yourself:
If I had those doubts, what would
someone have to do to persuade me?
What would I need?

*An effective persuader puts themselves in
the other person's shoes to give themselves
a better idea of the concerns and needs. This
gives them more ideas on how to persuade
the individual.*

WHO DO THEY RESPECT?

Show them how other people are already effectively doing what you are proposing, especially people they respect.

If an individual can see that someone like them is already doing a particular thing, it can be reassuring and persuasive.

USE A GROUP TO HELP YOU

Work in numbers. If you can find a group of people who will support you, ask the other person for support when they are with this group.

People will usually go along with the crowd, even just to fit in.

HANDLING THEIR DOUBTS

If they have doubts, show them that you had doubts to start with too (if this is truly the case!), but that you changed your view because of the benefits or reasoning behind the new idea.

The best persuaders will sometimes make the other person's doubts seem like a natural part of the journey to acceptance.

JUMPING HURDLES

If they put obstacles in your way, ask them a question to keep the conversation moving and to put the ball in their court. E.g. ask "What would need to happen for us to go ahead with this?" or "what would need to happen for you to get this sorted by Friday?"

People like to have their needs considered and when asked for their ideas, they will often begin to champion your cause.

THE RESCUE QUESTION (1)

Stuck? If the other side not prepared to
play fair...
Try the rescue question:
"If we can find a way forward that
works for both of us,
are you prepared to help me find it?"

Seek to get everyone on the 'same side'.

THE RESCUE QUESTION (2)

Going round in circles?
Try asking them: "What do you need
here?"

*Focus on other people's outcomes as well as
your own.*

NO MORE YES BUTTERS

If someone keeps saying "yes, but…" to your ideas, ask them: "So, if we were to do this, how would *you* go about it?"

The effective persuader knows that sometimes people resist ideas because they feel that their own suggestions are not being heard.

THE PROBLEM WITH THAT IS...

If you are getting a problematic
response to your solutions...
(e.g. "the problem with that is..." or
... "the difficulty there is ..." or
... "the trouble with that is..."
You will first need to identify and
agree your outcomes,
(i.e. what you both want to achieve or
where you want to get to).
Then seek solutions (i.e. how to go
about it).

*It is easier to find solutions to outcomes
than it is to problems!*

BUILD A BRIDGE

If the other person's idea is different to yours, but has some good points in it, you could build on the good part of their idea, and then move it towards your own.

A good persuader will start with the other person's point of view and then build connections. The other person will often end up thinking that the final result was their own idea anyway.

THE CULTURAL EXCHANGE

Consider the culture of the person
you are dealing with.
Are they more direct or indirect?
Straight to the point or dance a little?

*Where possible, respect cultural differences
and match the communication style of the
other person.*

**BUILDING
LIKE AND TRUST**

BE UP FRONT

Avoid trying to trick people into liking and trusting you. Think of being likeable as a way of life as opposed to a quick fix technique.

The effective persuader understands that a good relationship is based on sincerity and integrity.

BUILD EMPATHY

Build empathy for your cause by
asking them:
"Put yourself in my shoes, what would
you do?" or "If you were in my shoes,
how would you go about…?"
or "How would you feel if you were in
my shoes right now?"

*Empathy will often build a connection
between two people and make them more
receptive to finding mutual solutions.*

I LIKE YOU (1)

Help people to like you
by being likeable!
(This means not being rude,
unpleasant, sarcastic, cynical,
arrogant, aggressive, sycophantic,
cold, pushy… etc).
Listen to feedback that people give you
and observe their reactions to you.

*People are more likely to be persuaded by
someone they like.*

I LIKE YOU (2)

Take a genuine interest in people.
Listen to them. Find out more about
what they like. What and who are
important to them?

*Most people like to talk about themselves
and will feel charmed by a good listener.*

I LIKE YOU (3)

Smile, be genuine and friendly.
Make sure that people associate seeing
your face with a positive feeling.

*People are more likely to be persuaded by
someone who makes them feel good.*

REMEMBER THEM

Make a note to remember a person's name, their achievements and any other points of interest. Remember their birthday. Send them a card.

People not only like someone that remembers them, but they will remember that person too.

BUILD TRUST

Be a friend. Be there for people. Put people first above all else.
As you discover information about them, reveal similar information about yourself.

People are more likely to believe and trust a friend.

GIVE A LITTLE

Be prepared to give something in order
to get what you want...
"If I was to need X from you, what
would you need from me?"

Playing fair can help seal the deal!

CONNECT

During conversation, find out and talk about what you share in common. What is similar about your interests, beliefs, backgrounds…?

The more people have in common, the more they can relate to one another.

PERSONALISE

Use the person's name
(but in moderation).

*People are more likely to be persuaded if
they feel that you have personalised your
idea to them.*

ATTRACTIVENESS SELLS

When you want to persuade, dress well and make yourself look as attractive as you can!

People are more likely to help and buy ideas from attractive people. Sad but true.

THE ART OF NODDING

If you want someone to agree with you,
build rapport and gently nod
as you speak.
If they start nodding too,
make your request.

When others nod and we like them,
we tend to nod too!
It is harder to say "no" to someone when
you're nodding!

SEEK TO HELP OTHERS

Do something spontaneously for someone. Help them (when they need it) without their prompting.
Do these things without expecting anything in return.

People remember kindness and will often tell others. They will tend to be more receptive and willing to return the favour some day (even if simply to "level the playing field").

USERS ARE LOSERS

Avoid only contacting people when you want something from them. Give as well as take.

People switch off to others if they feel they are being used.

BUILD COALITIONS

In group situations, support people verbally if and when you agree with them.

When openly supported, people often feel a sense of coalition and will support you later (when it matters to you).

PUBLIC ANNOUNCEMENT

Acknowledge other people's input to
your success in a public way.
Tell other people about how helpful
that person has been.

*When acknowledged publicly, people are
more likely to support and help you again.
Also, other people may want to share in
your successes by helping in the future.*

PRAISE

Praise people for what they do well rather than criticise them for what they don't do so well.

People are motivated by praise and acknowledgement.

A NOTE OF THANKS

When someone helps you, thank them personally. Perhaps show your appreciation by writing them a hand-written note or a card.

People rarely throw away a sincere and personalised written note of thanks that they receive. They remember it because it is unusual in these "modern times".

SPECIAL AND DIFFERENT

Tell them you would value their input
and involvement.
When asking for help from someone,
tell them why you are asking *them*
specifically. Compliment them (but
avoid obvious flattery).
"You're the main person I trust to ask
for help on this…"

*People will often help if they are made to
feel special or indispensable.*

INVOLVE THEM

Ask the involve question:
"If you were doing this, how would
you go about..."

People do not tend to reject their own ideas.

DISCUSS AND SHARE

Instead of giving people advice and
expecting them to take it, discuss issues
and ideas with them.
Ask: "What do you think?"
(Remember that the danger of giving
people advice is that they might just
take it!)

*People are more likely to buy into
a shared idea.*

CONSULT THEM

Involve the other person in decisions. Work together to find a way forward that suits everyone.

People feel more committed to an idea if they have been consulted and involved.

WHAT I LIKE IS...

If you are in a discussion where there are conflicting ideas...
Find something you like about their position.
Tell them what you like and *then* put your proposal forward.
E.g. "What I like about your idea is that it gives us x...
my idea will also give us y...
perhaps we can find a way forward to get both x and y?"

When faced with potential conflict, effective persuaders will seek innovation... and true 'win/win' solutions.

ON THE TEAM

When persuading, consider yourself and the other person to be part of a team, working together on a solution that is good for the team.
Imagine what will happen when **you are on the same side**!

The fundamental principle behind any relationship is always to remember that you are both on the same side.

GAUGE THEIR VALUES

Match your idea to their personality.
If they like exciting, make your idea
sound exciting.
If they like safe, make your idea
sound safe.
What is important to them?

*The most experienced persuaders gauge the
other person's values and sell their idea
based on those values.*

USE THEIR LANGUAGE

It is essential that you step into their world and use their language. Mirror back key words and phrases they use in their conversations. It will make it easier for them to understand your idea if you talk in their language.

People like other people who are like them (even if they don't like themselves!) as it is safe and familiar.

OBSERVE BODY LANGUAGE

Watch their body language.
Is it similar to yours?

When two people get on well, their body language, movement and tone of voice become very similar.

REACTIONS

When you suggest something, watch the other person's facial expression. The immediate reaction is likely to tell you what they really feel and think. However, remember to place their reaction in context of what else is going on. Trust your gut reaction and test your hunches.

People reveal a lot about how they feel through their body language and voice tone. It is usually expressed and read at an unconscious level.

OI CHEEKY!

Read the situation and build rapport.
Act appropriately but be prepared to be
a little cheeky!

*Sometimes the 'art of influence' is simply
asking for what you want!*

TWO-WAY TRAFFIC

Avoid making the poor persuader's
mistake:
"If I talk at them for long enough, then
they'll see it my way!"

Effective persuasion usually requires a two-way interaction.
Telling may gain compliance but involvement will gain commitment.

ASK QUESTIONS AND LISTEN

After asking a question, be silent.
Really listen rather than thinking about
what you want to say next.

*Have you ever found yourself in
conversation where you are speaking or
waiting to speak? Where is the space for
listening?*
*(And have you ever noticed that "listen" is
an anagram of "silent"!)*

CHOOSE TO LISTEN

When you are with someone, say to
yourself:
"I need to listen to this person".
You will find that you pick up and
remember much more information.

*Consciously choosing to listen increases
focus, concentration and memory.*

LESS INTERRUPTING

Let the other person have their say
without too many interruptions
from you.
If trying to resolve a conflict, listen to
them and their story first. Work to
understand what they need.

*The best persuaders know that if they don't
listen to the other person, the other person
has no reason to listen to them.*

SHOW INTEREST

Take an interest in the other person.
Ask them about who they are, what
they do and what they like.
You may learn more about what you
have in common (which gives you a
better chance of persuading them).
They may even reciprocate and take
more of an interest in you.

*The successful persuader works to build a
relationship by finding common ground to
build upon.*

CO-OPERATE

Offer your support to them in the spirit of co-operation.
For example: "If I was to need this doing by Friday, what would you need from me?"

The successful persuader gets to know people, building long term relationships where there is some give and take over time.

MAKE MANY FRIENDS

Get to know and make friends with as
many people as you can.
You never know when you may be able
to help one another <u>and</u> you never
know who they may know!

*If you know 100 people and they all know
100 people, then you have potential access
to up to 10,000 people!*

BUILD A PROFILE

Build up a positive profile and
reputation for being likeable,
trustworthy and good at what you do.

*60-70% of success is down to: "who that
matters knows what that matters about
you".*

KEEP PROMISES

Build trust over time by keeping
promises and being
truthful and honest.
Then you can say:
"Have I ever let you down?"

*Solid trust takes time to build, but people
are strongly persuaded by consistency.*

COMMUNICATE

Tell people what they need to know up front and then keep them informed of developments, updates and changes. Keep them "in the loop".

Without solid information, people will make up what they think is going on and then believe that instead.
Education, information and communication go a long way towards persuasion.

INCREDIBLE!

Build credibility over time by demonstrating your knowledge and expertise.
Publish your successes. It is possible to let people know about your achievements without seeming "too big for your boots".

People are more likely to be persuaded by someone who has demonstrated a successful track record.

A WARM DRINK

If seeking agreement and rapport, offer the other person a hot drink rather than a cold one.

Research suggests that when holding a warm drink, people judge others as more generous and caring!

PRESENTING
YOUR CASE

WHAT'S THE POINT?

Explain your idea clearly and give reasons as to why it's a good idea. Explain the purpose of your idea – what is the point of it? What is the aim?

People tend to be more open to an idea if they understand what it is and why it needs to be done.

GIVE THEM REASON

How about giving them a reason to
listen to your idea?
E.g. "I've had an idea that could save
us money."
Associate your idea with a positive
feeling before you have even told them
what it is!

*People are more likely to listen if they think
that an idea may benefit them.*

THE BIGGER PICTURE

Show them how what you are proposing fits into the bigger picture.

When an idea is demonstrated to fit into a person's long-term plan, they are more likely to accept it.

W.I.F.T.
(WHAT'S IN IT FOR THEM)?

Remind people what they may lose if
they don't take action as well as what
they may gain by taking action.
What's in it for them?
What are the benefits to them if they
change or move to accept your idea?

*People are ultimately motivated away from
pain & loss and towards pleasure &
benefits.*

PROS AND CONS

Some people need to hear the benefits
of an idea...
Some people need to hear the
consequences of no action...
And some people need a little of both.

*When there may be a cost of
not taking action,
be prepared to communicate this
as well as the benefits.*

CREATE A GAP

If you want someone to be receptive to your new idea, you need to show them what is wrong with things as they are. This creates a "gap" for you to slot in your idea.

When people feel dissatisfaction or doubt with the present, they are more open to a new idea that could provide a better future.

THINK LONG TERM

What are the long-term benefits if your idea is followed?
What are the long-term negative consequences if your idea
is not followed?
Demonstrate how following your idea could prevent certain problems
from arising.

People like to feel secure about the future.
They want to feel that there is
happiness ahead.

UNIQUE?

Use the marketing professional's approach:
What is the unique selling point of your idea?
What makes it special and different?
Why is it better than the alternatives?

People like to think that they are buying into something that is exclusive, special and better than the rest.

BUILD UP YOUR IDEA

Consider...
...how following your idea
will help them.
...how it could save or make
them money.
...how it could save them time in
the long run.
...what other opportunities your idea
could bring.
...how your idea is a safe and secure bet.
...how it could improve
the quality of their life.
...how it could make things easier
for them.

*When someone feels good about an idea,
they are more likely to be persuaded by it.*

PICK OUT THE BEST BITS

Avoid overselling your idea where the
benefits become more and more
insignificant.
Stick to the key benefits and number
them as you express them.
E.g. "There are three main benefits.
Number one is…"

*A small number of strong benefits is much
more persuasive than a lot of weak ones.*

MAKE A POSITIVE FIRST IMPRESSION

Although this has become a bit of a cliché, it <u>is</u> important to make a positive and confident first impression. It will affect how everything goes from that moment on.
People will judge your suggestions based on what they think of you.

Numerous studies have shown that decisions are made about other people within the first few seconds.

SPEAK WITH CONFIDENCE

Use a confident tone of voice.
What does this sound like?
Listen and emulate strong positive
speakers from television, radio and
everyday life.

*People's voices, when confident, are deeper,
constant in pitch and speed, clear,
appropriate in volume to the surroundings
so that they can be heard easily without
shouting.*

STOP GOING "UP"

Sound sure of what you are saying by staying level at the end of a statement. Avoid making statements sound like questions by going "up" at the end. Try saying "I'll give you ten pounds for it" by staying level at the end and then by going "up" at the end. What do you notice?

Saying a statement as if it is a question sounds uncertain and is less persuasive.

OPEN OR CLOSED?

Consider the difference between:
"Can we meet?" and "When can we meet?"
"Was this helpful?" and "How was this helpful?"
By turning a closed 'yes/no' question into an open one
(e.g. by using 'when', 'where' or 'who'), you can move a conversation beyond potential disagreement...

Effective persuaders seek to direct conversations and minimise the barriers.

REDUCE THE WEAK WORDS

Avoid weak words like: "possibly", "maybe", "don't know if" and phrases like: "this may be a stupid idea but…" or "you'll probably think this is silly but…"
If you don't believe in your idea, how can you expect others to?

Successful persuaders take their ideas seriously and sound like they believe in them.

SHOW THE FEELING

If you want people to feel excited about
your idea, you need to get excited
yourself.
If you want people to appreciate the
seriousness of a situation, you need to
take it seriously.

*People are more persuaded by others who
say things and sound like they mean it.*

A WEIGHTY ARGUMENT

If you need someone to take an idea seriously, give it to them in a heavy binder or on a weighty clipboard.

Research suggest that holding a heavier document brings with it feelings of seriousness and importance.

SHOW THE IMPORTANCE

Tell and show them how important this
idea is and why it is important
to them too.
Demonstrate how passionately or how
strongly you feel about it.

*People prioritise ideas. If an idea is really
important it goes to the top of their list.*

SHOW THEM THE BETTER FUTURE

If your idea is a good one, demonstrate your enthusiasm and build up the positive feeling by giving them a picture of a better future.
Tell them your vision of how it could/would be.

People like to have an idea of how it will turn out. Having something to work towards is motivational and therefore persuasive.

AID THEIR DESTINY

Show them how your idea fits with
their values and goals.

*People are more persuaded by an idea if it
seems like it will help them with their own
destiny.*

YOU, YOU, YOU!

Use the words "you" and "your" more than the word "I".

The words "you" and "your" may well be the most persuasive words in the English language.

YOU ARE ALREADY THERE

Tie your idea into something they already do or like.
E.g. "It's similar to what you are already doing, with some additional benefits."

People are more likely to be persuaded by an idea if they are already part way there.

THE BUYING ZONE

If someone has already "bought" an idea from you or someone else, sell them your new idea soon after this. As long as it is a reasonable idea, they are more likely to accept it.

When people are open to one idea, they are more open to other ideas too. They are in the buying "zone".
(People also do this with shopping – if they go into a shop with bags of stuff from previous shops, they are more likely to buy from this shop too.)

TIMING IS EVERYTHING

Present your idea, proposal or request
when they are in a good mood and a
helpful frame of mind.
Avoid trying to persuade them in the
middle of an argument.

*When people are happy, they are more open
minded.*

EXPERIENCE IT FOR YOURSELF...

If possible, let someone try out a product and/or hold it.

Research suggests that people have more confident feelings about something if they have interacted with it rather than just read about it.

IT'S ALL IN THE PACKAGING

Make your idea look and feel good.
Package it so that it is colourful,
irresistible, delicious, welcoming,
delightful, harmonious, fun,
entertaining…

*People will often buy an attractive box,
even if the box contains something
mediocre.*

EXCLUSIVITY

Make your idea sound as if it exclusive or scarce in some way.
E.g. not many people know this yet or there is a limited time-scale in which it can happen. This is the "window of opportunity" – "now or never"…

If people perceive that something is rare, they will want it even more.

EVERYONE ELSE IS DOING IT

If it is the largest selling or the fastest
growing thing, tell them.
If the rest of the world thinks it's okay,
it must be.

*People are persuaded by the "9 out of 10
people prefer our product" approach, partly
to fit in with the majority, but also because
it seems "tried and tested".*

THINK TALL

How do you come across when you are proud and confident?
Walk, stand, sit, think and live <u>tall</u>.

Confident people are perceived as being more successful and having more authority.

CERTAINTY? CERTAINLY...

Express yourself with certainty.
Stick to fact. Give concrete evidence
and real-life examples to back up what
you are saying.

*Those that are more certain are likely to be
the more persuasive.*

BECAUSE I SAY SO

Use the word "because" with reasons to back up your argument. It sounds more like fact than opinion.
As much as possible, avoid portraying opinion as fact because if someone catches you "bluffing", you will lose credibility.

The word "because" appears to be one of those magic words where people assume you have good reasons simply because you used the word "because"!

NUMBER YOUR REASONS

Put your reasons into a logical
sequence and number them.
Then present your strongest reasons
one by one.
E.g. "There are 3 main reasons to go
with this idea. Number one… etc"

*When reasons are numbered, not only does
it provide a clear structure, but also people
remember that there were a specific number
of reasons, even if they don't remember the
actual reasons!*

QUOTE STATISTICS

If it helps your case, quote statistics (as long as they can be interpreted to back you up).

Statistics can be interpreted in many ways, but if a statistic sounds reasonable, people will usually believe it.

SCIENCE

By saying: "Research demonstrates that..." followed by your argument, most people will take this at face value if it sounds reasonable (and sometimes if it sounds totally extra-ordinary!)

Our culture programmes us to consider scientists to be smart and usually right. Why doubt what a scientist says when they know more about it than we do?!

IF YOU SAY SO...

If you state a number of facts/truths in a row and people agree with them, they will often believe the next piece of information you give them, even if it sounds a little incredible.

It takes more thought and effort to disagree with what someone says, when you have agreed with everything they've said up to that point.

HOW DO YOU LIKE IT?

Some people appear to need to see
something to believe it...
some people need to hear it...
or read it...
or experience it directly in some way.

*Effective persuaders determine whether
they need to show, tell, write to, involve or
take a combination of approaches, in order
to convince someone else.*

HOW OFTEN DO YOU LIKE IT?

Some people can be convinced almost
straight away... others may need to
see/hear/read/experience it
a number of times.
Some people will be convinced if they
see/hear/read/experience something
over a period of time...
Whilst others seem to need to be
convinced over and over and over!

*Effective persuaders will be persistent with
those that are not convinced first time
around... because they understand it may
be a personality thing.*

THE POWER OF PRINTED WORD

Have things written down e.g. your ideas, solutions or plans. Type them up and print them if appropriate.
Then express your enthusiasm and certainty as you tell the other person about these ideas.

People tend to find written words more convincing and credible than spoken words. But they tend to find spoken words more emotive and motivational.

RATIONAL AND EMOTIONAL

Appeal to someone's rational side by
being factual and structured.
Appeal to someone's emotional side by
being motivational.

*People are both rational AND emotional
animals.*

GIVE AND TAKE

Is there anything that they want that you are prepared to give, in exchange for what you want?
Show them that you will support/help them with their idea if they help you with yours.

Negotiation is the oldest form of co-operation known to people-kind.

BE FLEXIBLE

In some areas of your proposal, be prepared to move a little bit yourself (especially if this leads to a result that suits you and the other person).

People respond like with like. They are more likely to be flexible if they see flexibility in the other person. They are more likely to be persuaded by someone who has worked <u>with</u> them on a solution.

HELP!

Ask for help with your idea.
Don't expect people to read your mind.
The worst they can do is say "no" –
then you are no worse off than you
were before!

*People cannot help you unless they know
you need help.*

WHO MAKES DECISIONS ROUND HERE?

When persuading, negotiating or seeking help…
find and speak to the decision maker whenever possible.

Persuading the wrong person can be a great time-waster!

IF AT FIRST...

If you are sure that you have
a strong proposal,
but it doesn't go your way first time...
be persistent!
Try again... try a different approach...
or try a different person!

*Effective persuaders rarely give up
first time!*

IF IT'S NOT WORKING, STOP PUSHING!

Ever seen someone try and open a door
by pushing when it is clearly marked:
"PULL"?
Don't just push ideas at people!
Be prepared to ask their opinion...
ask their advice...
ask what they think...
ask what they need...

*Effective persuaders engage others by
asking them questions.*

MAKE YOUR MIND UP –
TAKE YOUR TIME

If appropriate, allow them time to come
to terms with your idea.
Let them weigh it up for themselves.

*People will usually be more committed to
something if they have time to make their
own mind up about it.*

WHAT ELSE?

WHAT ELSE?

MAKE IT EASY FOR THEM

Show willing to do the leg-work.
Make it easy for them, hassle-free.
All they have to do is show up (or sign
on the dotted line…!)

*People will often be put off an idea if it
sounds like an effort.*

GIVE THEM
A NUMBER OF OPTIONS

Give them a choice of 2 or 3 options
that still give you what you need.
This way they feel involved and
consulted even though you have
generated the options.

*When people feel they have a choice, they
often don't notice that the options are
actually limited to a certain number of
outcomes.*

BE PERSISTENT

If all else fails, you could always use the kids' technique of asking over and over and over and over...

People sometimes admire persistence. Other people may simply want to get some peace and quiet and so give you what you want to get that!

AVOID IRRITATING THEM

Avoid obvious leading questions and
sales closes.
Avoid putting them down with
aggression and sarcasm.

Dislike is an instant turnoff to persuasion.

DO SOMETHING DIFFERENT

If you get stuck for ideas or for a way
forward, do something different.
Talk to a new friend or colleague.
Go for a walk and visit places you have
never been to before.
Drive home a different way.
Shop at a supermarket you don't
normally go to.

*The brain needs to be awoken and
stimulated in order to be creative and come
up with new ideas.*

ASK THEM FOR THE BENEFITS

If you are feeling cheeky, ask the other person to list the benefits of your idea. "How might it help you if we were to…"

When a person starts listing the benefits of your idea, they are pretty much persuaded!

BREAK IT DOWN

If you are asking for a big favour, break it down into bite-size chunks that are easier to agree to.

Once people start agreeing with small, reasonable requests, it is hard for them to know when to say "no" without seeming inconsistent.

ONE STEP AT A TIME

If someone thinks that they would have to change their mind to accept your idea, remember:
There is no such thing as a change of mind, merely a progression of thought!

Effective persuaders will often persuade on a step by step basis, rather than expect the other person to make a big change immediately.

BOUNDARIES...

Handling a person who is being
disrespectful?
Try something like:
"I want to work with you here,
I want to help you...
but not like this."

Effective persuaders stay courteous and
helpful... even in the face of rudeness!

OTHER OPTIONS:
DEFER OR REFER?

If you feel 'put on the spot',
can you *defer* part of your conversation
till later?
Alternatively, can you *refer* part of your
discussion to someone else.
(e.g. "I'll need to speak to
Fred about this.")

*Effective persuaders know <u>when</u>
to address issues they can't immediate
answer and <u>to whom</u>.*

HANDLING BIG EGOS

If you are dealing with an ego, let them
think it was their idea (as long as you
get the result you are after).
Ask their advice on how they would
go about doing what
you want to get done.

People with large egos seem to think all
good ideas were theirs. And if they think
the idea was theirs, they won't reject it.

LABEL IT

If someone asks you to do something
for them, label it "a favour":
"Okay, I'll do it for you as a favour."
It is easier to get them to help you later
by calling in the favour.

*When something is labelled it becomes more
concrete. Most people don't like to seem
unreasonable by not returning a concrete
favour.*

SAYING "NO" (1)

Remember that if you need to say "no" to a request, the "asker" will usually be able to find help elsewhere. They may even have a mental list of people to ask.

People take the "path of least resistance". If you have always said "yes" in the past, guess who they will come to next time!

SAYING "NO" (2)

If you need to say "no", you could say:
"I'm sorry, but no, I'm not in a position
to... (whatever they have
asked of you)."

A straight, confident and pleasant "no"
will be accepted by most people.

I CANNAE TAKE
ANY MORE CAP'N!

Getting overloaded by requests from
the same person (e.g. a manager)?
Try responding something like:
"I'm happy to do it but am currently
working on this...
Which would you like me to do first?"

*Understanding other's priorities can go a
long way to managing their expectations.*

NO NAGGING!

If the other person "never seems to get round to it", avoid 'nagging' because this will build up resentment and frustration.
Talk with them, not at them. Find out their concerns and resistance and then help them to overcome the resistance. E.g. by sharing the load with them or giving them something in return.

The best persuaders understand that persuasion is usually a two-way process.

DEADLINES

If things drag on, set a solid deadline; let the relevant people know about it and then stick to it.

People are often motivated by specific deadlines. Indeed, a task without a deadline is a clear invitation for procrastination.

ENVIRONMENTAL FACTORS

If you want someone to be kinder, softer and more malleable in their approach, have them sit in a soft, comfortable chair and/or in contact with soft material.

Research suggests that people tend to be less rigid and harsh if the environment is comfortable (as opposed to e.g. sitting in a hard or rough chair).

DRESS FOR WHERE
YOU WANT TO GO

If you are looking to enhance your career, dress for the job you want and not the job that you have already got.

The successful persuader will wear clothes that "match" a status or role. This makes it easier for them to join the new "club" because other people find it easier to accept someone like themselves.

LEARN, LEARN, LEARN!

If it doesn't go to plan and success is
not immediate, be persistent!
Look at what happened, talk it through
with a friend and then decide how you
will approach things
differently next time.

*Persuasive people learn from their
"mistakes" and work out new strategies for
the future.
The most successful persuaders have taken
more risks and had more "failures" than
the least successful persuaders.*

IF NOT YOU... WHO ELSE?

If you cannot change the situation
yourself, who else can?
Identify those that might be able to
influence the situation
and find a way to influence *them*.

Grow your circle of influence by finding
those with the power to make the change.

A FINAL WORD

Remember:
Persuasion brings no guarantees;
it simply increases your odds of getting
a result.

*Be optimistic... **and** realistic!*

ABOUT THE AUTHORS

Joe and Melody Cheal have been involved in the Personal & Professional Development fields since 1993, gathering best practise from all walks of life and business. They have personally trained and coached over 20000 people, helping them revolutionise the way they interact and work with others.

They have been married and happily influencing one another since 1994!

Joe Cheal

Joe is the Lead Imaginarian and Trainer for Imaginarium Learning & Development. He has been involved in the field of management and organisational development since 1993. In focusing his training, coaching and consultancy experience within the business environment, he has worked with a broad range of organisational cultures, helping thousands of people revolutionise the way they work with others.

He holds an MSc in Organisational Development and Neuro Linguistic Technologies (his MSc dissertation was an exploration into 'social paradox'), a degree in Philosophy and Psychology and diplomas in Coaching and Psychotherapy.

Joe is an NLP Master Trainer who enjoys learning new things… by exploring diverse fields of science, philosophy and psychology and then integrating these 'learnings'. He is the author of *'Solving Impossible Problems'*, *'Who Stole My Pie?'* and the co-author of *'The Model Presenter.'* He is also the creator and editor of the ANLP Journal: *Acuity*.

Melody Cheal

Melody lives on the edge of Ashdown Forest, East Sussex with her husband, Joe and two dogs. She has a degree in Psychology, an MSc in Applied Positive Psychology, a diploma in Psychotherapy and is an NLP Master Practitioner and Certified NLP Master Trainer. She is a qualified Hypnotherapist and Hypnosis Trainer.

She is part of the external verification panel for the ANLP accreditation programme. Her Psychological Approaches to Coaching Diploma is accredited by the Association for Coaching.

She regularly speaks at national conferences and has presented her dissertation research, 'NLP and self-esteem', at an international research conference. Her work was published in an academic journal as a result. She is the author of *'Becoming Happy'* and the co-author of the popular book, *'The Model Presenter'*.

LEARNING & DEVELOPMENT

Imaginarium Learning & Development is a consultancy that specialises in inspiring the natural potential of organisations, leadership, management and individuals through OD, L&D and Executive Coaching.

We work with clients from a broad range of sectors and aim to work in partnership with our clients, enhancing the profile of leadership, learning and development in our client's organisation.

Since 1993 we have experience of working with thousands of people from many organisations including:

Aeroflex, Amnesty International, ARA (Aircraft Research Association), Astra Zeneca & AstraTech, Autoglass, Avondale, Balfour Beatty, Bedford Borough Council, Central Bedfordshire, Beds Health, Beds Magistrates Courts Committee, Belron, Bio-Products Laboratories (BPL), Birdlife and Plantlife, British Gas, BT, Calderdale Council, Cambridge City Council, Cambridge University Press, Camelot, Cellnet, Central Bedfordshire, Church Conservation Trust, Cranfield University, Dixons Stores Group International, Emmaus Village Carlton, GSK, Herts Magistrates Courts Committee, Hertsmere Borough Council, Inland Revenue, J. Murphy & Sons, Langley Search & Selection, Lockheed Martin, London Borough of Camden,

Luton Borough Council, Mercedes AMG High Performance Powertrains Ltd, Mylan, Newham Council, North Herts District Council, OAG, Olympic Blinds, RSPB, Sainsbury's, Santander, Serco, Shepherd Stubbs Recruitment, Staverton Park Conference Centre, The Assessment Network, Tesco, University of Hertfordshire, Welwyn Hatfield Borough Council, Welwyn Hatfield Community Housing Trust, Willmott Dixon, The Wine Society.

Imaginarium offers a range of consultancy services including:

- Training courses
- Executive coaching and skills coaching
- Facilitation and team development
- Change management, Organisational development and Learning & Development consultancy
- Strategic engineering and Paradox management
- Myers Briggs profiling and Emotional Intelligence testing

Why work with Imaginarium?

Here are 4 things that make us special…

Experience
Imagine tapping into a wellspring of experience to help your people become more effective, more efficient and even more resourceful.

We have been involved in the learning & development environment for a quarter of a century! In the training and coaching environment, we have encountered and understood the majority of problems and challenges that human beings can face. We are able to draw from a wealth of practical resources, solutions, examples, models, hints, tips and ideas to help get people unstuck (and to help them 'unstick' themselves!) As individuals, we continue to learn and develop, keeping what we do fresh and engaging. We 'get' people!

Credibility
Imagine working with a company who regard your success and credibility as highly as their own.

We value not only our own credibility but also the credibility of the company we work with. We know that when we are training and coaching in your company, we represent "learning & development". We are passionate about advancing the reputation and culture of people development in organisations. We have worked with a vast range of organisational sectors and cultures giving us the ability to adapt from one company to another. We have also worked with some highly multicultural organisations, from people from all across the globe.

Humour & Enjoyment

Imagine your staff… keen to develop themselves to become even better at what they do.

We love what we do! People who train with us enjoy themselves. We've been told that some people laugh and smile more in one day than they normally do in a week! We believe that enjoyment and light-heartedness are one of the most important keys to learning. Wherever we have embedded into an organisation's culture, people want to attend courses!

Return on Investment

Imagine working with people who care that their service adds measurable value.

It is important to us that whatever we do, it adds value for your company. Sometimes this can be realised in terms of financial profits and savings. Sometimes return on investment is subtler in terms of staff motivation, efficiency and improved communication. Whether the returns are tangible or intangible we are keen to make sure that we are worth our weight in gold!

Our courses and topics include:

LEADERSHIP DEVELOPMENT
Change Management
Coaching Performance
Delegate!
Feedback for Effectiveness
Making Meetings Work
Management Development Programmes
Managing People Successfully
Mentor Skills
Motivate!
Project Leadership
Team Building and Development

RESULTS AND RELATIONSHIPS
Assertiveness: Clarity and Focus
Building Partnerships
Communication
Conflict Resolution
Customer Care
Dealing with Aggression
Dealing with Difficult People
Handling Conflict in Meetings
Influence and Persuasion
Magic of Mediation
Negotiation Skills
Understanding Personalities

IN FRONT OF THE AUDIENCE
Advanced Presentation Skills
The Essential Presenter
Persuasive Presentations
Train the Trainer

PERSONAL IMPACT
Career & Profile Development
Coping with Change
Dealing With Pressure
Innovation: Getting Creative
Managing Your Performance
Staying Positively Happy
Stress Management
Time Management

EXECUTIVE DEVELOPMENT
Advanced Negotiation Skills
Becoming a Mentor
Beyond Selling
Making NLP Work
Managing Tensions
Organisational Development
Organisational Politics
Storytelling in Business
Strategic Change Management
Troubleshooting: Problem Resolution
Working with Transactional Analysis

HR SKILLS FOR MANAGERS
Appraisal
Capability & Disciplinary
Controlling Absence
Dealing with Poor Performance
Introduction to Counselling
Managing Difficult People
Recruitment Selection & Interviewing
Tackling Bullying & Harassment

Psychological Approaches to Coaching Diploma

Accredited by the Association for Coaching

The programme is designed to allow learners time to reflect, consolidate and practice between modules. Each module is three days in length and includes supervised coaching practice with feedback.

For experienced coaches there is the opportunity to dip into the programme and attend individual modules. As this course is accredited by the Association for Coaches the modules can be used as CPD.

The modules are:
- Foundations in Coaching
- Transactional Analysis for Coaches
- Using the iNLP Coaching frame work
- Positive Psychology Coaching

GWizNLP

Training in Neuro-linguistic Programming (NLP)

NLP (Neuro-linguistic Programming) could be described as the psychology of excellence and the science of change. Through understanding more about how the mind/brain works (neuro) and how language affects us (linguistic), a practitioner is able to initiate and sustain change (programming) on a personal, interpersonal and organisational level.

NLP was designed originally to model excellence. By establishing exactly how someone achieves something, excellence can be modelled, taught to someone else and repeated again and again. From this starting point, over the last thirty years, an array of processes, concepts and techniques have been developed to enable you to:

- become more resourceful in managing attitudes, thoughts, emotions, behaviours and beliefs
- relate to others easily and effortlessly,
- understand how language and its use has a direct impact on your state, your brain and your success in communicating with others.

In addition to all this, as a GWiz NLP practitioner, you will learn techniques designed to help you develop your own skills and help others develop theirs. The principles will be introduced conversationally and with activities throughout the course allowing you to learn on many levels consciously and unconsciously.

As NLP Master Trainers we offer the complete three levels of certified NLP courses throughout the year:

- NLP 101
- NLP Diploma
- NLP Practitioner
- NLP Master Practitioner
- NLP Trainer's Training

We also offer Accredited Hypnotherapist training from entry level through to Hypnosis Trainer.

As part of the ongoing support offered to all our students Melody provides supervision groups, mentoring and personal support to our graduates. This support is available to practitioners trained elsewhere.

If you are interested in personal and professional development and would like to more about NLP, have a look at our website: www.gwiznlp.com or contact us: info@gwiznlp.com.

Becoming Happy!
Lessons from Nature

By Melody Cheal

The search for happiness can often seem elusive and so this book provides hope for those wanting help in becoming happy.

Find out how to unlock the best version of you, recognising your own sense of worth and value. Melody shares experiences from her own journey of self-discovery plus tools and ideas she uses in her own practice.

The combination of pictures drawn from nature plus simple easy to apply exercises provides the reader with tools to begin transformation.

Are you ready to Be Brilliant?

WHO STOLE MY PIE?

By Joe Cheal

How to manage priorities, boundaries and expectations

Walter's lunch... and his time are being eaten into.

Fortunately, 'real-world' help is at hand to help him manage his time... and inadvertently, his pies!

Join Walter in learning how to manage priorities, boundaries and expectations...

Make your life easier and more fulfilling!

Who Stole My Pie is packed with powerfully simple models, tools, tips and techniques. If you want to gain greater control over your time then this book is for you!

Other Books from GWiz Publishing

the
MODEL
presenter

By Joe & Melody Cheal

The Model Presenter will show you how to:
- Develop the qualities of an exceptional presenter
  - Create a memorable and logical structure
  - Deliver presentations and training with confidence.
  - Engage an audience easily and effortlessly
- Deal with a wide range of challenging situations

This 'how-to' guide is filled with steps to follow and helpful hints and tips modelled on the best of the best.

You will discover a host of original material including:
* Closing the Gap between yourself and the Mind of the Audience
* Preparing using the BROADCAST Model
* Delivering training sessions using the IMPACT Formula
* Transforming nerves into confidence

Be remembered for the right reasons…
*As you become **the Model Presenter**!*

Other Books from GWiz Publishing

SOLVING
IMP⊘SSIBLE
PROBLEMS

By Joe Cheal

Say goodbye to organisational dilemmas, tensions, conflicts and stress with
Solving Impossible Problems.

The ability to manage tensions, paradox and uncertainty in business is becoming a much sought after leadership skill.
'Paradox Management' is a new but increasingly essential field in the area of business management and will be highly influential in the ongoing sanity and success of all organisations and of the people who work for them.

Solving Impossible Problems will give you a greater understanding of organisational tensions and paradox. You will learn how to recognise these 'twisty turny' problems and then use practical tools to resolve them or use them for innovation.

*This book is a unique guide to heightened wellbeing and enhanced thinking power through the revolutionary process of **Paradox Management***.

For more information about
Joe & Melody Cheal,
Imaginarium Learning & Development
and/or GWiz NLP,
you can contact us at:

E: info@imaginariumdev.com
E: info@gwiznlp.com

Ph: 01892 309205

W: www.imaginariumdev.com
W: www.gwizNLP.com

Lightning Source UK Ltd.
Milton Keynes UK
UKHW02f0421060118
315642UK00006B/145/P